My Calm-Down Books

I CAN BREATHE

Caitie McAneney

PowerKiDS press

PK Beginners

Sometimes I feel sad.
Sometimes I feel mad.

My heart beats fast.
I want to yell or cry.

Big feelings are hard.
What can I do?

I can find my calm.
Calm means peace.

I can breathe
to calm down.
My breath is a tool!

11

I breathe in.
I make my
belly bigger.

I breathe out.
I make my
belly smaller.

15

I keep breathing.
I start to feel better.

17

My heart slows.
My body settles.

19

I can deal
with my feelings.
They are not
hard now.

I am calm.
I can do anything—
one breath at a time!

23

Published in 2024 by The Rosen Publishing Group, Inc.
2544 Clinton Street, Buffalo, NY 14224

First Edition

Editor: Caitie McAneney
Book Design: Rachel Rising

Photo Credits: Cover, p. 1 Yuliya Evstratenko/Shutterstock.com; pp. 3, 11 fizkes/Shutterstock.com; p. 5 Sharomka/Shuttestock.com; p. 7 Krakenimages.com/Shutterstock.com; p. 9 FamVeld/Shutterstock.com; p. 13 kornnphoto/Shutterstock.com; p. 15 Torychemistry/Shutterstock.com; p. 17 Khosro/Shutterstock.com; p. 19 Khorzhevska/Shutterstock.com; p. 21 Dmytro Zinkevych/Shutterstock.com; p. 23 Yurii_Yarema/Shutterstock.com.

Cataloging-in-Publication Data
Names: McAneney, Caitie.
Title: I can breathe / Caitie McAneney.
Description: New York : Powerkids Press, 2024. | Series: My calm-down books
Identifiers: ISBN 9781642824889 (pbk.) | ISBN 9781642824896 (library bound) | ISBN 9781642824902 (ebook)
Subjects: LCSH: Breathing exercises--Juvenile literature.
Classification: LCC RA782.M45 2024 | DDC 613'.192--dc23

Manufactured in the United States of America

Some of the images in this book illustrate individuals who are models. The depictions do not imply actual situations or events.

CPSIA Compliance Information: Batch #CSPK24. For further information contact Rosen Publishing at 1-800-237-9932.

Find us on